A HISTORY
OF ST MAWES
SAILING CLUB

Nigel Sharp

AMBERLEY

First published 2016

Amberley Publishing
The Hill, Stroud
Gloucestershire, GL5 4EP

www.amberley-books.com

Copyright © Nigel Sharp, 2016

The right of Nigel Sharp to be identified as the
Author of this work has been asserted in accordance
with the Copyrights, Designs and Patents Act 1988.

ISBN 978 1 4456 5299 3 (print)
ISBN 978 1 4456 5300 6 (ebook)

British Library Cataloguing in Publication Data.
A catalogue record for this book is available from
the British Library.

Typeset in 9.5pt on 12pt Celeste.
Typesetting by Amberley Publishing.
Printed in the UK.

Introduction

This book was never intended to be a *complete* history of St Mawes Sailing Club. It simply couldn't be, partly because of lack of space, but mainly because there are so many gaps in the records and knowledge of the club's past, particularly the early days. No one knows, for instance, the names of any Commodores from when the club was formed in 1920 until 1928.

The village of St Mawes must have been ready for a sailing club in 1920. St Mawes Regatta (now St Mawes Town Regatta) is known to have been held as early as 1842, and possibly even earlier; the Royal Cornwall Yacht Club had been formed in 1871 and Falmouth Sailing Club in 1894, although the latter had closed by the time the First World War broke out; the first five boats of the Falmouth 18 Foot Restricted class had been built (three of them in St Mawes) around the turn of the century and had been racing throughout Falmouth harbour ever since, and an eighteen-year-old Frankie Peters was starting to build boats at his family's long-established boatyard at Freshwater.

It was also in 1920 that Frank Green designed and built a 14-foot centreboarder called *Nesta* for himself, and three more for other local sailors. The fact that these boats appeared at the same time that the club was formed can hardly have been a coincidence, and it is generally thought that Frank and the owners of the other three boats – Miles Brown, Colonel Ernest T. Harden and Dr T. Bashall – were among the founder members of the club, along with Harry Douglas Harden, Joanna Tracey, Dr Arthur Preston, Les Ferris and Frankie Peters. The 2015 membership list includes descendants of at least three of those.

Major landmarks in the club's history include the acquisition of Stoneworks Quay in 1958, moving into a permanent clubhouse in 1977 and its expansion in 1985, and the formation of the Junior Sail Training programme in 1990. The importance of the foresight and resolve of the Commodores and committees of those times cannot be overstated and this is borne out by the ever-increasing membership figures, which have reflected the club's improving facilities and opportunities. There were 194 members in 1939 and the effects of the Second World War do not seem to have been too disastrous in that respect as there were 197 in 1947. From then on, each decade has shown a steady but impressive increase: there were 334 members in 1955, 759 in 1965, 865 in 1975, 1,104 in 1985, 1,298 in 1995, 1,574 in 2005 and 1,765 in 2015.

The content of this book has been largely determined by the photographs and accompanying information that I have been able to find and which have been contributed by a number of StMSC members and others, to whom I am extremely grateful. With this in mind, I very much hope that no one will be aggrieved by the absence of any photographs or stories about them, their loved ones, their boats or any members who have made significant contributions to the club.

Around the time that StMSC was formed, Frank Green (one of the founder members) designed and built a 14-foot gunter-rigged boat called *Nesta*. Three other boats – *Crazy*, *Bombay Dick*, and *Mevagissey Goose* – followed soon afterwards and these four boats raced under the club burgee on Wednesday afternoons and were, at that time, known as the St Mawes One Design class. This photo shows *Nesta* with Frankie Peters at the helm. (StMSC Archive)

In 1923, Frankie Peters designed a 16-foot gunter-rigged boat called *Aileen* (pictured above in 1924) having been beaten by a Dr James in club races, probably when sailing one of the 14-footers. *Aileen* soon got the better of Dr James and was so successful that Frankie was asked to build other boats to the same design. At some point these boats collectively became known as the St Mawes One Designs, putting the 14-footers in the shade. To date forty-five of the 16-foot One Designs have been built – most of them at Freshwater Boatyard (twenty-four by Frankie, one by Brian Crockford and thirteen by Jonathan Leach) – and forty-one are known to have survived. (StMSC Archive)

The above photo shows a fleet of gunter-rigged St Mawes One Designs racing off Falmouth Docks. This would have been taken before 1953, the year that the class converted to Bermudan rig and added 20 square feet to the sail area. All classes tend to come and go in terms of their popularity, and the St Mawes One Designs are no exception. At the beginning of the 1980s they had been suffering something of a decline, until a wonderful revival, largely led by Andy Tyler whose own boat was No. 29 *Vesper*, resulted in some impressive turnouts over the next two decades: twenty boats in Falmouth Town Regatta in 1986 for instance, twenty-three in St Mawes SC Regatta in 1987, twenty in Falmouth Week in both 1993 and 1994, twenty-four taking part in a sail-past and nineteen in a race to celebrate the seventy-fifth anniversary in 1998, and twenty-five in the eightieth anniversary race in 2003 – thought to be the largest fleet ever. The photo below was taken during the sixtieth anniversary race in 1983. (Both photos StMOD Archive)

It was in 1924 that the first eight Sunbeams arrived in Falmouth, by railway, a year after a fleet had been established on the Hamble River. Throughout the class's early years, most of the fleet crossed the Carrick Roads to compete in StMSC's weekly races, and the photo above shows seven of the original boats starting one such race. Exhaustive research of race records reveals that it is impossible to pinpoint the date of the photo, but it was definitely taken before 1928 and most probably in 1924, that very first season. Just two of the original eight boats – V14 *Halcyone* (now V38 *Tantivy*) and V21 *Maranui* – are still based in the Falmouth area while the others are at Itchenor. From the mid-1950s until the mid '70s, the majority of the Falmouth Sunbeam fleet was based in St Mawes and for many years a dozen or more boats would be guaranteed to cross the StMSC start line twice a week. The photo below was taken in August 1987.
(The Harden Collection and Jerome O'Hea)

Frankie Peters was the fourth generation of the family that designed and built boats on the banks of the Percuil River. His great-grandfather William Peters started building boats in St Mawes in 1790 and is generally acknowledged as the world's first builder of Pilot Gigs, and Frankie's grandfather John and father Nick followed in William's footsteps. Some of their gigs were exported throughout the world. Frankie made his own mark in the nautical world, however, as a highly skilled boat designer, builder and sailor. He is pictured above at Freshwater Boatyard with Joe Andrew and Willum Andrew in 1953, and below in retirement, when he spent a great deal of time using his extraordinary skills making model boats. (StMSC Archive and the Peters Collection)

There have only ever been nine boats in the Falmouth 18 Foot Restricted Class, which has just one measurement rule: that the hulls must be 18 feet long. This photo shows *Magpie* and *Marie*, which were built in St Mawes by Fred Pasco in 1898 and by Frankie Peters in 1930. *Magpie* was originally gaff-rigged but was converted to Bermudan soon after *Marie* was built. During the late 1940s and '50s their owners – George Corke of Mylor and Frankie Peters – enjoyed an intense rivalry, racing each other up to five times a week, often with extraordinarily close finishes. This attracted huge local interest in St Mawes where, it is said, 'the whole village' would turn out to watch them. (StMSC Archive)

Five 18s survive today and in recent times all have been based at St Mawes and sail with gaff rigs. Four of them – *Myrtle* (built 1902), *Moey* (2010), *Whisper* (1981) and *Magpie* – are seen here racing off St Mawes in 2010. Only *Marie* is missing. (Nigel Sharp)

It is unusual for any centenarian boat to have survived without, at some point, falling into a state of disrepair before the intervention of luck and an enthusiastic new owner. The two oldest 18s are no exceptions and these two photos show *Magpie* and *Myrtle* before they were rescued by StMSC member Duggie Burnett and restored by John Fuge.
(Both photos the Edwards Collection)

It is thought that these photos were taken just before (above) and just after (below) the First World War. Not only do they include the building in which StMSC would eventually establish its own clubhouse in 1977, but they also show some of the places, or approaches to those places, where the club had the use of various facilities before that: at the Victory Inn, for instance, in 1939; and in 1948 at the Ship and Castle Hotel. Throughout the late 1950s and early '60s, StMSC member Bert Sawle was the proprietor of the St Mawes Hotel and, according to the yearbooks of the time, kindly gave 'wall space for a large notice folder, and other facilities'. In 1947, club secretary Miss Carlisle allowed the use of her home, Landfall, which, according to a newspaper report, had 'a balcony overlooking St Mawes harbour and having an excellent view of the start, finish and of a considerable proportion of the sailing course', although it isn't clear where Landfall was. At various other times there were notice boards outside the Steamer Office (the building immediately to the left of the Ship and Castle Hotel) and in the early 1970s outside the National Westminster Bank (just to the right of the Victory Steps).
(Both photos St Just and St Mawes Heritage Group Archive – SJSMHG)

In 1923 Charlie Ferris bought the gaff cutter *Edith*, which then remained in his family for around seventy years, and was most notably used by his son Les to teach sailing and to take people out on fishing and pleasure trips. Other boats that Les used for teaching and hiring included *Whim*, *Myrrh* and the St Mawes One Designs *Kelpie* and *Nymph*. Les was a StMSC committee member for well over thirty years, and served as both Vice Commodore and Rear Commodore. These photos show him teaching in *Edith* (above) and in *Kelpie* (below).
(SJSMHG Archive and the Ferris Collection)

Before the war there were only two nationally established dinghy classes: the International 14 and the National 12. Both were (and still are) development classes, which provide opportunities for different designers legitimately to exploit the measurement rules. In 1934, Frankie Peters designed and built an International 14 called *Moonyeen* (pictured above) for Ian B. Henderson. That summer Ian entered her for the Prince of Wales Cup, the annual race that decides the class's national champions, with Frankie crewing for him. In a fleet of forty-one boats, they came fourth, a result which brought great acclaim for Frankie in the press. 'Considering that her opponents included the product of some of the most eminent builders of International dinghies, this was a remarkable achievement,' read one report. (The Peters Collection)

Three years later Frankie designed and built a National 12 called *Kingfisher* (pictured right) in which he finished second in a highly competitive National 12 fleet in the Coronation Regatta in Torbay. (The Peters Collection)

Another StMSC member who competed in that same POW Cup race in 1934 was Joanna Tracey, a founder member of the club, with her husband Christopher crewing for her. They finished just one place behind Frankie and one place ahead of Stewart Morris (eventually a twelve-time POW Cup winner and Olympic gold medallist). Joanna also owned and sailed the Sunbeam *Binaiya* (now *Ivy*) from before the war until 1957 and was a regular, and often successful, competitor. The photo above shows *Binaiya* having a scrub on Summers Beach in the early 1950s. In 1984 – when their respective sons Nick and Richard were about to sail to the Caribbean together – Jim Tresidder asked Joanna (then aged eighty) to helm his Sunbeam *Verity* in St Mawes Regatta. She did and they came second in a fleet of sixteen boats. (The Tracey Collection)

Jim Tresidder (StMSC Commodore from 1999 to 2002) helming *Emily Too* in the 2006 Marieholm Championships. (The Howard Collection)

St Mawes Town Regatta was firmly established a long time before StMSC was formed – it is known to have been held in 1842 and may well have started long before that – but the club has, for many years, provided much of the infrastructure for the sailing races. Furthermore, in 1924, the *Falmouth Packet* reported that the aquatic sports were held under the auspices of StMSC and that 'crowds of people lined the pier and the event proved very popular, particularly the blindfolded praam race ... a dance was held in the Memorial Hall in the evening, when a magnificent gramophone, standing six feet high, provided the music.' The above photo was probably taken in 1910, while the one below shows the rowing races taking place in the harbour in 1937. (SJSMHG Archive and Vivien Sharp)

Very little is known about this photo but it was almost certainly taken just after the start of a race at St Mawes. The gaff-rigged boat in the centre of the photo may well be *Kaanoge*, which was owned by Dr Penrose (Commodore 1946–1949) from soon after the war until 1967; the Bermudan-rigged boat just ahead of her might be General Costin's *Felicity*, which he owned for about twenty-five years, and the boat to windward and just aft of her is probably Philip Sharp's Tumlare *Jinny the Queen*. (The Banner Collection)

Philip and Richard Sharp – at that time a past and a future Commodore – sailing their Firefly *Sabrina IV* in the Percuil River in the 1950s. The first time a Firefly appeared in St Mawes was in August 1946 when the prototype was lent by the manufacturers Fairey Marine to StMSC members Lieut-Cdr and Mrs J. S. Carlisle. (Vivien Sharp)

In October 1958, StMSC acquired Folley Cellar Quay (otherwise known as Stoneworks Quay) from the Public Trustee for £400. In the late nineteenth century the quay had been owned by the Coverack & Polvarth Stone Company Ltd, which extracted stone from Dean Quarry, near Coverack, and transported it to St Mawes in three Thames sailing barges whose flat bottoms allowed them to sit on the shallow foreshore adjacent to the quay for unloading. The stone was probably used for road-building on the Roseland. These photos looking at the quay from across the Percuil River were taken shortly before the First World War (above) and sometime in the 1920s (below). (Both photos SJSMHG Archive)

Soon after the acquisition of Stoneworks, its existing building was rented out to two club members before it was demolished in 1961. The same year, after permission was granted by Cornwall Council and the Ministry of Transport, the slipway was built. These photos show various club members taking part in working parties at that time.
(Both photos StMSC Archive)

These photos of Stoneworks Quay are thought to have been taken in late 1961, and show the small shed, which was built around the same time as the slipway, as well as three Sunbeams and an 18 Footer (probably *Marie*), which were laid up there. (Both photos StMSC Archive)

In the winter of 1998/99 the small shed on Stoneworks Quay was demolished. These photos show work beginning on the larger building that replaced it – to accommodate toilets, showers, an engine shed, a training room and other storage areas – and which still exists today. (Both photos StMSC Archive)

Major Alec Matthews has been the longest-serving Commodore of StMSC, occupying that office from 1949 to 1961. Throughout that time, and indeed up until 1970, he owned the Falmouth Sunbeam *Harmony*. He is seen above chasing *Bubbly* and *Lindy* (which are probably being helmed by John Sawle and Bruce Cocking respectively) in a brisk south-westerly, and (below) sailing on a much calmer day with his family: his grandchildren Ian, Anne and Brian, all of whom are now Fifty-Year Life Members of the club, and his son Peter on the helm.
(The Sawle Collection and the Matthews Collection)

Between 1965 and 1967, Alec Matthews also co-owned *Tern IV* – the 62-foot yawl designed by and built for the esteemed nautical writer Claud Worth in 1924 – with Tony Black, another Sunbeam owner. Club member Jo Shaw (née Colson) did her first offshore race in her, from Helford to L'Aberach in 1966, with Alec and his wife Betty, the paid-hand Alan Huntley, and her parents Hugh and Moy. She clearly remembers the calm conditions after the start (which allowed them all to enjoy steak and peas sitting in deck chairs), the strong winds and horrendous seas later in the voyage, and the three days of partying in L'Aberach. The picture to the left shows *Tern* completing a Falmouth to Fowey passage race, and the one below reflects Alec's generosity in frequently taking young StMSC members sailing. Those pictured include Robert Wilson, David Royall, Mickey Horsfall and Ginny Milne, while Alec keeps a lookout to starboard. (The Shaw Collection)

Before the current race office on the top floor of the clubhouse came into use in 1987, StMSC's races were run from the quay. According to the company's own records, in 1947 the St Mawes Pier & Harbour Co. 'granted the St Mawes Sailing Club permission to erect the Club's "flagpoles and marks" on the Quay as in former years (i.e. years before the War)' and in 1966 'agreed to the parking of a caravan on the quay at a fee of £17 for the seventeen-week period'. These photos show two teams of race officials on the quay. The photo above was taken before the days of the caravan, possibly in 1958, and includes (left to right) Stanley Green, Dennis Edmonds, Ralph Day, G.F. Marrecco, Joy Teasdale (now Joy Matthews and, in 2016, the longest-serving member of StMSC) and Major Alec Matthews. The photo below shows Dougie Sawle (left and partly hidden), Tony Fisher (middle) and Brenda Pye (middle right) in front of the caravan, and is likely to have been taken in 1984 when they were Race Officer, Sailing Secretary and Rear Commodore Sailing respectively.
(The Banner Collection and the Fisher Collection)

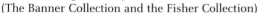

The caravan can also be seen in the bottom right of this photo, which was probably taken in 1971. (The Pridmore Collection)

St Mawes One Designs crossing the club's start line at the beginning of a race to celebrate the class's sixtieth anniversary in 1983. (The Carden Collection)

In June 1977, under the leadership of the then-Commodore Michael Dover, StMSC purchased a two-bedroom flat above St Mawes Post Office from Barclays Bank. Thanks to a great deal of hard work by a number of members, by the beginning of August this had been converted to a clubroom and bar. The entrance was in Commercial Road, through a narrow passageway and up the stairs, which are now the club's fire escape. This photograph shows the hatchway that formed the bar at that time with Glenn Litherland in the foreground. (StMSC Archive)

In May 1985 the club purchased the first and second floors of the adjacent premises to the south-west, which had been Melanie's Gift Loft with a flat above. This immediately allowed the club a greatly improved main entrance facing the quay and a great deal more space. This made room for a new bar, which is pictured above with Howard Lees – who had spells as both Vice Commodore and Rear Commodore House – manning it. (The Sawle Collection)

By 1987 a race office (more or less overlooking the same start line that the club had already been using for many years) was established on the top floor of the newly expanded premises. The top photo shows the balcony from where races are now signalled (in this case for Junior Race Week in 2014) and the one below is looking the other way, along the line, at the Working Boat start in St Mawes Town Regatta in 2013. (Both photos Graham Pinkney)

Enterprises were once very popular at StMSC: sixteen boats took part in one club race in 1964, for instance (some of them helmed by well-known members such as David Bucknell, Henry Ferris, Jo Colson, Keith Ferris, Peter Matthews and Richard Tracey), and the following year a total of twenty-eight different boats raced at the club. The above photo was probably taken during a regatta, while the latest sail number (5076) in the photo below determines that it was taken after 1975, although it appears to be much older than that.
(Mark Osborn and the Banner Collection)

Hugh and Moy Colson joined StMSC in 1950 and Hugh subsequently served on the committee for more than twenty years, including spells as Hon. Secretary, Rear Commodore and Vice Commodore. This photo shows Hugh and Moy in their Redwing *Sevallack* in the 1950s. The Redwing was a popular class at StMSC at that time: nine of them took part in a club race in September 1954, for instance. (The Shaw Collection)

After *Tern IV* was sold the Colsons started sailing on Bob Church's Nicholson 32 *Jane Waterman* and then his Nicholson 35 of the same name. They bought the larger boat (pictured left, dressed overall) from Bob in 1984 and they are thought to have completed more than twenty-five French cruises on her. (The Shaw Collection)

In May 1969 an Ajax – number 43 *Astrid* belonging to Harold White – raced at St Mawes for the first time. Three years later Michael Dover brought *Hermes* to St Mawes and it was from then that the class developed. By 1980 there were twenty-eight boats registered with the Falmouth Ajax Association. Just thirteen of those were owned by members of StMSC but over the subsequent years more and more of the fleet came to be based on the St Mawes side of the water. For thirty years or so the class's annual National Championship has been held alternately in Falmouth/ St Mawes and Harwich (where the only other UK fleet is based) and in non-Nationals years a South-West Championships is held. The Ajax fleet has repeatedly achieved impressive turnouts over the years: twenty-nine boats in Falmouth Week in 2005, for instance, and twenty-five in the 2006 Championships. These two photos show the starts of Championship races in very contrasting conditions, in 2013 (above) and 2014 (below). (Both photos Graham Pinkney)

Among the people who have dominated the Ajax class is David Matthewson in *Ajax* (pictured above with his wife Kim and Trudy Rosevink crewing for him in the 2006 Championships). *Ajax* won Falmouth Week in 1992, for instance, and then three years running from 1994; the Nationals in 1995 and 1996, and twenty-five out of thirty-five StMSC points races in 1993. (The Howard Collection)

In 1996 David Liddington joined the Ajax fleet when he bought *Athena* and he soon began an extraordinarily long period of domination. He won Falmouth Week eleven years running from 1997 to 2007, and then again in 2009 and 2010, and he won the National Championships five times – the first time, in 2005, in Harwich, and then in 2006, 2008, 2010 and 2014. He is pictured here during the 2014 Championships with his son Paul and Rob Geddes-Brown. (The Howard Collection)

Marieholm International Folkboats were all built in Sweden between 1968 and 1978. The first one to arrive in St Mawes, in the mid-1980s, was *Zeitgeist*, but it wasn't until the early to mid-nineties that the class became established here after early proponents of the class – including John Todd, Christopher Hoare, Jim Tresidder, Robert Iselin and Brian Roberts – actively sought available boats throughout the UK and beyond, not just for themselves but for other local potential owners. At one time, when only twenty Marieholms were known to exist throughout the country, thirteen of them were based in St Mawes.

In 2000 the Marieholm National Championships were hosted by StMSC for the first time and have been every year since. Brian Roberts won three of the first four Championships in *Teide* before Charles Warren and his family won it five years running, and again in 2012 and 2013. Bridget and Alan Macklin have won the last two Championships, as well as the last five Falmouth Weeks, in *Annika*. These two photos were taken at the 2014 Championship: *Tringa* leads at the start above, and *Mathilde* goes a different way to the rest of the fleet below. (Both photos Graham Pinkney)

From 2001 to 2010, the Marieholm and Ajax classes held their Championships jointly, but since 2011 the Ajaxes have had their own event and the Marieholms have combined with other classes: initially the Falmouth 18 Foot Restricted Class and subsequently the International One Designs and Nordic Folkboats as well. These photos were taken at the Marieholm/18 Footer Championship in 2011: *Otter* chases *Tringa* and *Annika* above, and representatives of both classes are shown below. (Both photos Graham Pinkney)

In the late 1980s David Muirhead discovered the original St Mawes One Design, *Aileen*, near Chichester. The Class Association raised funds to buy her and bring her back to St Mawes to be restored by Jonathan Leach. The above photo shows her being relaunched at Freshwater Boatyard on New Year's Day 1989 with Frankie Peters and Jonathan standing next to her bowsprit; and the photo below shows Jonathan and David sailing her up river for the start of Percuil Regatta in August 2003. (StMOD Archive and the Carden Collection)

The photo above shows *Aileen* after the start of the 2003 Percuil Regatta and on her way to Falmouth, where she was donated by the Association to the National Maritime Museum Cornwall. The photo below shows a small armada of One Designs, which gathered at the museum to mark the occasion. (Both photos the Carden Collection)

Freshwater Boatyard has been owned and run by various StMSC members throughout the lifetime of the club, and has provided an essential service to countless other members.

Frankie Peters owned and ran the yard from around the time the club was formed until he retired in 1962, when it was taken over by John Sawle. Bob Houchin purchased it in 1969 and he employed Brian Crockford (until 1974) and then Willum Andrew to run it for him. Duggie Burnett and John Green took it over in 1974 until 1983 when they sold it to John and Fran Castle. John served as the club's Commodore from 1988 until 1992, and in 1997 he decided to sell the yard. At that time the club considered buying it 'as a service for boat owners, and as a centre for the club sail-training operation it might draw substantial grant aid' according to the then-Commodore Brian Davis. But it was not to be and it was soon sold to Mike and Sue Thomas who ran it until 2011, and since then it has been in the hands of Mark Humphrey. The date of the photo above is unknown but it was presumably taken long before the one below, which is dated 1910. (Both photos StMSC Archive)

The above photo shows Willum Andrew, Frankie Peters and Joe Andrew at Freshwater Boatyard in 1953, and the one below shows the yard in 1960, since when it has been considerably developed. (The Andrew Collection and StMSC Archive)

Helford Maid was one of the Lion class, designed by Arthur C. Robb and built in 1952 at Falmouth Boat Construction. Bernard Liddington bought her in the early 1970s and she was then based in St Mawes until soon after his death in 1985. During that time *Helford Maid* rarely sailed without Stanley Drinkwater, either as crew or as skipper in Bernard's absence. This photo clearly shows Stanley standing up and leaning against the boom. (The Liddington Collection)

Philip Sharp – Commodore 1946 – sailing his Tumlare *Jinny the Queen*, which he owned from 1938 to 1983. Several more of these Knud-Reimers-designed double-enders have been based in St Mawes over the years including *Kestrel, Ariadne, Astra, Sabline, La Paloma, Sabrina, Zest* and *Tinkerbell*. (The Sharp Collection)

Two classes taking part in StMSC's Regatta in the days when the Carrick classes started from a committee boat line off St Mawes; Optimists in 1983 and part of the fleet of sixty-nine Flying Fifteens in 1997. (Nigel Sharp and Mark Osborn)

Since the middle of the nineteenth century, oysters have been harvested by sailing vessels in the upper part of the Carrick Roads and there is still a by-law in force that prevents oyster fishermen from using engines. There was a time when the same gaff cutters – the Falmouth Working Boats as they have come to be known – that dredged in the winters also raced in the summers, but nowadays the two fleets are more or less separate. Each year StMSC hosts a number of races for the Falmouth Working Boats including the World Championships – the word 'World' is slightly tongue-in-cheek but few would argue that the winner isn't the best Falmouth Working Boat in the world – and the St Mawes Harbour Race. These photos were taken during the Harbour Races in 2007 and 2015. Five B Class Working Boats are currently based in St Mawes. (Both photos Nigel Sharp)

Florence is the oldest of the St Mawes-based Working Boats. She was built in 1895 by William 'Foreman' Ferris in Pill Creek and has spent much of her life oyster-dredging and fishing at sea. In 1965 her then-owner lent her to John Sawle – a member of StMSC and at that time proprietor of Freshwater Boatyard – who then raced her with great success for a decade or so; in 1969, for instance, *Florence* won all six races in Falmouth Week – a feat that has never been equalled in the Working Boat fleet – and in 1970 she won eighteen prizes. During this time she captured the hearts of the people of St Mawes, some of whom, it is said, raised money at coffee mornings to help pay for new sails. After that she went back to dredging, but in 1997 she was purchased by the newly formed St Mawes Working Boat Syndicate. Among the founder members of the syndicate, and still in it today, are three descendants of the man who built her: Andrew, Shaun and Colin Ferris.

These photos show her being raced by John Sawle and his crew in the late 1960s (above) and by the syndicate in 2015 (below). (The Sawle Collection and Nigel Sharp)

Florence getting ready to race in the 1960s with (left to right) Jack Cannon, John Sawle, Warwick Kendall, Horace Hodges, Dennis Hitchings, Ronnie Harris and Butch Gay on board. (The Sawle Collection)

This photo shows the St Mawes Syndicate and friends celebrating *Florence's* 120th birthday in St Mawes harbour in August 2015. (Nigel Sharp)

Evelyn was built by Frank Hitchens in 1898 in Restronguet Creek and she has much in common with *Florence*. She is owned by another St Mawes-based syndicate, the Roseland Working Boat Syndicate, which was formed in 1994; she spent much of her life working before coming to St Mawes, and two syndicate members – Malcolm and Mark Hitchens – are descended from her builder. *Evelyn* won the first Falmouth Working Boat World Championships in 2005 and she won it again in 2012. The last *Evelyn* owner to use her for oyster-fishing was Kenny Corke and the above photo, probably taken in the 1970s, shows him sailing up the Carrick Roads to start another dredge. The picture to the left shows her racing past Pendennis Castle in 2010.
(The Evelyn Collection and Nigel Sharp)

Demelza has been based in St Mawes since 2002 when John Andrew – a former Rear Commodore Sailing of StMSC – bought her. She was built in GRP in 1973 and she, too, has won the World Championships twice, in 2008 and 2015. She is seen here sailing past St Anthony's Lighthouse on her way to Fowey in 2012. (Nigel Sharp)

Helen Mary – built in GRP in 1970 – has been based in St Mawes since 1996 and was mostly skippered by Dougie Clode until 2013, when Kevin Andrew took over. Falmouth Working Boats are only allowed to race with spinnakers on the passage races to and from Fowey and during Fowey Week itself, and this photo shows *Helen Mary* making the most of the opportunity on the way to Fowey in 2012. (Nigel Sharp)

The newest St Mawes-based Working Boat – in terms of both her year of build and her arrival in St Mawes – is *Mabel*. She was built in timber in 1985 and Brian Chenoweth bought her from Peter Collett – the then-Commodore of the Royal Cornwall YC, who had owned her from new having completed her construction – in 2013. This picture shows her racing past St Mawes Castle in 2015. (Nigel Sharp)

Falmouth Working Boats taking part in the 2014 St Mawes Harbour Race. (Graham Pinkney)

In 1987, under the leadership of Commodore Brenda Pye, StMSC hired a small fleet of Optimists from the RYA on two occasions to provide lessons for local children. The exercise was repeated over the following years – and in 1989 the boats came with an RYA instructor – but it wasn't until 1990, when steps were taken to purchase some boats, that the club's Junior Sail Training programme really got under way. This resulted from a conversation between Brian Roberts and Roger Smith, who both agreed that a proper training programme for local young people was essential for the club's future. Brian then set about raising money so that a fleet of eight Oppies could be purchased, and they are seen here sailing out of St Mawes harbour the following year.

Seven years later six Picos were acquired (pictured below on the harbour beach) and since then the club's dinghy fleet has been regularly replaced and added to. Since 1991 the club has owned over sixty sailing dinghies. (Both photos StMSC Archive)

Many people have made huge contributions to the development of the Junior Sail Training programme over the years, including Jim Tresidder, Arthur Melluish, Mark Osborn, Mike Croft, Heather Coutts-Wood, Annabelle Sylvester and Bob Warren, who was the Principal for ten years. In 2000 the club became an official RYA Training Centre, which allowed it to issue RYA certificates to trainees. In 2012 Bob Hindmarsh was recruited as the first full-time seasonal Training Manager, and later that year the club was awarded RYA Volvo Champion Club status in recognition of its active junior race training programme in RS Fevas. This was presented by double Olympic gold medallist Sarah Ayton to Mike Croft and eleven of our junior sailors at a ceremony in Truro (see photo below).

In 2015, in addition to Bob Hindmarsh, the club employed two Senior Instructors, seven Dinghy Instructors, fourteen Assistant Instructors and six RYA coaches who provided instruction to over 200 children who attended JST courses.

(Mark Osborn and StMSC Archive)

JST trainees who have gone on to greater things include Chris Thomas, who won the club's Desmond Sinnott Memorial trophy 'for racing progress' for the second time at the age of thirteen in 2007. He then teamed up with Jack Hawkins and in 2009 the two of them won the RS Feva Nationals and came sixth in the Europeans. They progressed to a 29er – in which they were second in the RYA Youth Nationals – and then to a 49er. In 2013 they were selected for the RYA Podium Potential Squad and a year later Chris carried the British team flag at the ISAF World Championships in Santander. These photos show Chris at the JRW prizegiving in 2008 (second from the left with Jack on his left) and sailing the 49er with Jack.
(The Osborn Collection and the Thomas Collection)

Will Richards learnt to sail at the club and went on to become a JST instructor. He is pictured here with HRH the Princess Royal, President of the RYA, when she presented him with the prestigious RYA Community Award (Youth Category) at the 2007 RYA AGM in recognition of his work 'as a very confident and professional sailing instructor with an enviable depth of practical and theoretical knowledge'. (The Osborn Collection)

A fleet of Fevas racing in 2013. (The Osborn Collection)

There have now been four bars (including the original hatchway) in StMSC's current clubhouse. The photo above is of the third bar before it was removed during the extensive refurbishment of 2011 and the one below shows boatbuilder Jonathan Leach constructing its replacement. (StMSC Archive and Graham Pinkney)

These two photos were taken after the 2011 refurbishment and, in the one below, Glenn Litherland – who has been a Flag Officer of the club for a total of eleven years, having had two spells as Rear Commodore House and another as Rear Commodore Sailing – can be seen sitting in the centre more or less in front of the position of the original hatchway.
(Both photos Graham Pinkney)

In their working days a number of Falmouth Pilot Cutters were based in St Mawes, including F8 *Vincent*, which was built in 1852 for William, John and Joseph Vincent, a family of pilots who lived in the village.
(The Sharp Collection)

In 1977 StMSC members Adam and Debbie Purser bought a newly built Pilot Cutter replica and named her *Eve of St Mawes*, and have been operating her as a skippered charter boat through their company, Classic Sailing, ever since.
(Nigel Sharp)

In 2006 Classic Sailing and StMSC organised the first Pilot Cutter Review, a series of weekend races and social events. Just four Pilot Cutters took part but each year it became increasingly popular, with fifteen boats – five of which were built before 1912 – attending in 2013 when these photos were taken. The boat below is *Merlin of Falmouth*, which was built locally at Cockwells Modern and Classic Boatbuilding in 2010. (Both photos Nigel Sharp)

In June 1990, the surviving past
Commodores of StMSC were invited
to attend the unveiling of the new
Commodores' board in the clubhouse.
Those present included Geoff Gibbs
and Brenda Pye (both pictured right
with the future Commodore Jim
Tresidder taking photos behind them),
Richard Sharp, Denis Clive, Mervyn
Harrison, Michael Dover, and Philip
Sharp (pictured below with Frankie
Peters and the then Commodore John
Castle, with the board about to be
unveiled behind them).
(Both photos StMSC Archive)

In 2001 the General Committee decided that anyone who had been a StMSC member for fifty years would be awarded Life Membership 'to recognise this achievement and high degree of loyalty'. This 2008 picture shows seven Life Members in the same family, all proudly wearing their special Fifty-Year ties and scarves. It was taken on the ninety-fifth birthday of Vivien Sharp (whose husband Philip was Commodore in 1946), and she is surrounded by her children: Richard Sharp (Commodore 1974–1975), Bridget Rumley, Nigel Sharp (Commodore from 2011), Tamsin Somers, Pip Farmiloe and Jennie Martin. Their combined membership at that time totalled more than 415 years. At the end of 2015 the club had twenty-seven Fifty-Year Life Members. (The Sharp Collection)

Honorary Life Membership is a more prized honour and is conferred on those members who have made a significant contribution to the running of the club. This photo shows the then-Commodore Brenda Pye presenting Dougie Sawle with a club burgee when he was awarded Honorary Life Membership in 1986. Dougie served on the General Committee for twenty-three years, with spells as Vice Commodore and Rear Commodore, and he was the club's permanent Race Officer for ten years. At the end of 2015 the club had ten Honorary Life Members. (The Sawle Collection)

Andy Tyler joined StMSC in 1979 and his boundless energy and enthusiasm were an inspiration to a great many people at StMSC and in the wider local sailing community. Without him, it is extremely unlikely that the revival of the St Mawes One Design Class in the early 1980s, the creation of both the *Evelyn* and the *Florence* Working Boat syndicates in the mid-1990s, and the Finn class's decision to hold their 2012 Gold Cup in Falmouth would ever have happened. Sadly, the latter took place a year after his untimely death. He is pictured above sailing on *Jambo*, when she was owned by his great friend Glenn Litherland, and below on his own GK24 *Duellist II*.
(Both photos The Tyler Collection)

StMSC ran a twenty-four-hour race for St Mawes ODs in 1984, and again in 1985. In 2015 it was planned to partly re-enact these races by running an overnight twelve-hour race but a bad weather forecast forced the race officers to shorten it to an evening four-hour race. These pictures were taken just after the start, and when some crew members were brought ashore after one of the crew changes. (Both photos Nigel Sharp)

Both these photos show Ajaxes sailing in their 2004 National Championship.
(Both photos the Howard Collection)

The Shrimpers have had their own class start at StMSC since 1998. The following year there were twenty-seven members of the club owned Shrimpers, and thirty-five in 2003. Thirty Shrimpers competed in Falmouth Week in 2001 and twenty-nine in 2004. In 2004 club member David Dorrell spent thirty-eight days sailing round mainland Britain (mostly single-handed) in his Shrimper *Humpol*. In 2012 ninety boats took part in Shrimper International Week – a series of fun events with just one day of racing – in the Fal Estuary. These photos show some of that fleet racing in the Carrick Roads (above), and moored up at Freshwater Boatyard. (Both photos Nigel Sharp)

It was in 2003 that StMSC first arranged its regatta day entertainments on the quay in front of the clubhouse. It has continued every year apart from two since then, and has typically included live bands, a bar, a barbecue and, on a couple of occasions, a big screen showing live pictures of the racing, accompanied by a particularly knowledgeable commentary from then-Commodore Bomber Holm and Andy Tyler. These photos were taken on Regatta Day 2015, and show club members and visitors gathering on the quay in the late afternoon (above), and enthusiastic volunteers getting ready to serve food from the barbecue (below). (Both photos Nigel Sharp)

Regatta teas have been provided by StMSC for a lot longer than the quay entertainments and have gained a great reputation among Falmouth Week competitors from all over the port. For many recent years the team of (mostly) lady volunteers has been led by Karen Richards, but this photo shows Mo Durnford and some of her helpers – the preparation complete and the serving about to begin – in 2015. (Nigel Sharp)

The start of a Handicap Yachts Class at StMSC's Regatta in 1983. (Nigel Sharp)

The International One Design is essentially a one-design 6-Metre, which was designed by Norwegian Bjarne Aas in 1936. The class established itself in St Mawes in the early 2000s when StMSC members began to purchase boats from the Clyde. Since then a total of seven different boats have sailed from St Mawes, forming the only UK fleet. Since 2008, StMSC teams have competed in various international IOD events, including World Championships in San Francisco, Sweden, Bermuda and Maine. In 2010, StMSC hosted the North Sea Cup, a biennial regatta involving fleets from Sweden, Norway and the UK.

These photos show IODs sailing in the local Championships: (above, left to right) *Happy Go Lucky*, *Wild Goose* and *Kyla* in 2006, and (below) *Greyhound*, *Kyla* and *Wild Goose* in 2014. (Rupert Scott and Graham Pinkney)

These photos show Ajaxes competing in their National Championships in 2006 (above) and 2014.
(Both photos the Howard Collection)

For the past ten years or so, StMSC has taken part in the annual RYA Onboard Feva Frenzy team-racing weekend at Siblyback Lake. In 2014 three StMSC teams (pictured above) competed against seven others from all over Devon and Cornwall, and the top two finished second and third, and in 2015 two StMSC teams (pictured below) took part and went one better, with the top team winning overall. (Photos Mark Osborn and Benny Hallam)

Up until 2002, StMSC had organised, for many years, an annual one-day junior regatta. But that summer, as a result of a conversation between Mark Osborn and a few parents, Junior Race Week was held for the first time. It was initially hoped that around ten juniors might take part, but nineteen turned up on the first day and by the end of the week the numbers had swelled to thirty. Since then the event has got bigger and bigger: fifty-one juniors in 2003, ninety-nine in 2008, and in 2013 a record was set with 120. However, this included a new afternoon Youth Racing Class and the following year the newly created Falmouth Dinghy Week (run by Restronguet SC in conjunction with StMSC) superseded that. Eighty-five juniors took part in Junior Race Week in 2015. These 2014 photos show pre-race rigging at Stoneworks Quay (above), and the Feva fleet rounding a mark (below). (Both photos Mark Osborn)

Pre-start manoeuvres in Junior Race Week 2013. (Mark Osborn)

The Memorial Hall has played a part in StMSC's history over the years. The club held a treasure hunt in 1947 to raise funds for the Memorial Hall Fund and the AGM has been held there since 1960. In 2008, when the numbers of juniors taking part in Junior Race Week had grown to the extent that it was no longer possible to hold the briefing in the clubhouse, it was moved to the Memorial Hall and has been held there ever since. This photograph shows the 2015 briefing. (Nigel Sharp)

Junior Race Week ends with a prize-giving and barbecue, either on Summers Beach or on the quay in front of the clubhouse, normally depending on the state of tide. These photos show the competitors on the Summers Beach steps at the end of one of the early Junior Race Weeks, and the prize-giving getting under way in 2009. (Both photos Mark Osborn)

Fevas on a spinnaker reach off Tavern Beach in Junior Race Week 2013. (Mark Osborn)

Optimists in Junior Race Week 2013. (Mark Osborn)

The photo on the left shows Frankie Peters and Willum Andrew winning the Falmouth to Fowey passage race in the Sunbeam *Clary* in 1957. Having sailed much of the race in gale-force winds, they arrived much earlier than expected, so no one from the race committee was there to fire a finishing gun. The photo on the right shows Willum and Frankie with the haul of trophies they won in *Clary* the following year. (The Andrew Collection and the Peters Collection)

Wahine was one of two of the Falmouth 18 Foot class designed by Dr E. H. T. Harden. She was built in St Mawes in 1903 by Fred Pasco (a cousin of the St Just Pascos) above what was then a coal store and is now the Co-op. Sadly she is thought to have broken her moorings in Falmouth in 1978 and, as a result of the damage caused, her keel was removed for scrap and her hull was burnt. In this photo Teddy Harden, the designer's nephew, is at *Wahine's* helm with Joe Barnes and Frankie Peters crewing. Stoneworks Quay – before it was acquired by the club – can be seen on the right of the photo. (The Harden Collection)

The 18 Footers *Whisper, Moey* and *Myrtle* racing in the Carrick Roads in 2010. (Nigel Sharp)

The 18 Footer *Myrtle* sailing off St Mawes in 2010. (Nigel Sharp)

The 18 Footers *Magpie, Marie* and *Myrtle* taking part in their 2014 Championship. (Graham Pinkney)

Many StMSC members have enjoyed the spectacle of superyachts racing in Falmouth Bay in recent years. The first Pendennis Cup took place in 2008 and has been held every other year since then. *Adela*, the 55.5-metre schooner built at Pendennis Shipyard in 1995, has competed in three of these regattas and she is seen here (above) dwarfing *Boyers Shrimper*, from which Mark Osborn was watching the racing.

On 26 June 2012 the J Class raced in Falmouth Bay for the first time for seventy-six years. Three days later, after racing was cancelled in slightly controversial circumstances after all four boats had motored out into the bay, *Velsheda* – the only original boat taking part – went back into Falmouth to collect Princess Anne and Vice Admiral Sir Timothy Lawrence, who were on a private visit to the regatta's hosts, the Royal Cornwall Yacht Club. The photo below shows *Velsheda* sailing past St Mawes Castle with her royal guests on board. Three of the Js returned to Falmouth for another regatta in 2015.
(The Osborn Collection and Nigel Sharp)

A great many StMSC members welcomed HM Queen Elizabeth and Prince Philip when they visited St Mawes on 6 August 1977 as part of the Silver Jubilee celebrations. The royal couple arrived by car along Tredenham Road and were then collected from the harbour in a royal barge, which took them past hundreds of well-wishers on moored vessels and over to Falmouth where *HMY Britannia* lay waiting for them. (The Freeland Collection and SJSMHG Archive)

In 2014, the Rona Sailing Project's 62-foot schooner *Merrilyn* took part in the Falmouth-Greenwich Tall Ships' Regatta. The skipper was StMSC Commodore Nigel Sharp and among the sixteen crew were eleven teenagers who were also members of the club. The race itself took place between Falmouth Bay and St Catherine's Point (the southern tip of the Isle of Wight) and, on corrected time, *Merrilyn* came an unspectacular, though respectable, nineteenth overall and third in class. These two photos were taken in the days before the race start – the one above shows *Merrilyn* on a practice sail in the Carrick Roads and flying a large Commodore's burgee, and the one below is of the whole crew in Falmouth. (Photos Mark Osborn and Oliver May)

Before the race started, many well-wishers from StMSC took to the water to enjoy the spectacular Parade of Sail in which the mighty *Dar Mlodziezy*, the 361-foot Polish fully-rigged ship, led the forty competing boats from the Carrick Roads out to Falmouth Bay. The above photo shows *Merrilyn* just off St Mawes before the parade started. (Richard Sharp)

When the race finished, *Merrilyn* made her way up the Thames along with the rest of the competing boats. The photo above shows some of the crew meeting Sophie, Countess of Wessex (the Royal Patron of the Association of Sail Training Organisations) alongside *Merrilyn* at West India Dock. (Oliver May)

Young members of StMSC have regular opportunities for other sail-training adventures on the Falmouth-based ketch *Hardiesse*. After the war, Neville Jackson (Joe) Feather formed a charitable trust and acquired the Bristol Channel Pilot Cutter *Christabel* for the purposes of sail training, and in 1956 she was replaced by *Shearwater*. Joe was the manager of the St Mawes branch of Lloyds Bank and he established informal links with StMSC, enabling younger members to experience sailing aboard *Shearwater*, and in 1961 he became a member himself.

In 1971 *Shearwater* was replaced by *Hardiesse*, a new boat built from ferro cement, but it wasn't until 2001 that a more formal link with StMSC was established, when club member Brian Roberts became a trustee of the Falmouth Sail Training Ship charity, a position he held until Tim Lowe took over from him in 2015. Each year at least one training weekend and a seven-day cruise to Brittany are allocated to StMSC young members, and typically between ten and twenty take advantage of that. These photos show *Hardiesse* drifting in the Carrick Roads and sailing off Falmouth. (Both photos the Hardiesse Collection)

In 1990 the Rear Commodore House Howard Lees invited the coxswain and crew of the Falmouth Lifeboat to enjoy StMSC's hospitality on a Saturday just before Christmas, and this soon became an annual event. In 2014 club member Rob Matthewson spent eight months growing a moustache – 'full-on nine-and-a-half inches of prime handlebar banger,' as he later described it – which he had publicly shaved off at the club during Falmouth Week. In doing so he raised £500 in aid of the RNLI, and a cheque for this amount was presented on his behalf to coxswain Mark Pollard during the Christmas visit. These photos show the Falmouth Severn Class all-weather lifeboat *Richard Cox Scott* and the B Class Atlantic 75 inshore lifeboat *Eve Pank* leaving St Mawes after the 2015 visit. (Nigel Sharp)

In May 1987 StMSC members Robin and Pat Bowden set off from St Mawes on a round-the-world voyage in their Calisto 385 *Tournel of St Mawes*. Three years later, in May 1990, they returned and, according to then-Commodore John Castle, 'approached the line in spectacular fashion, surrounded by an escort of club boats'. The picture above shows them moored off St Mawes immediately before departure, and the one below shows them sailing on a subsequent voyage. (Both photos the Bowden Collection)

The photo above shows the Bowdens' earlier boat, the Rustler 31 *Tournel*, and the Tradewind 33 *White Rose of Lastingham* owned by their friends Mike and Diana Garside, moored off St Mawes on 1 June 1980. That day *White Rose* set off on a circumnavigation (initially in company with *Tournel*) with the Garsides' children Katie and Melanie on board, returning two years later. Mike and Diana both subsequently took part in round-the-world races: Diana in the 1996/97 BT Global Challenge, and Mike single-handed in the 1998 Around Alone. At that time the Garsides were not StMSC members but they joined in 2012 and Mike became Vice Commodore two years later. (The Garside Collection)

In June 2012, Katie Garside was about to set off on another circumnavigation – with her partner Chris and their children Dylan and Leili on their Westsail 43 *Iona* – when disaster struck after *Iona* broke her moorings off St Mawes in a storm and drifted onto Summers Beach. The photo above was taken the next day when an extraordinary rescue operation – involving a 300-tonne crane and many local people including Julian Davey, Robin Edwards and fishermen Peter and Andrew Green – succeeded in getting *Iona* afloat again with the minimum of damage. A few weeks later she was able to set off on her voyage. (Nigel Sharp)

Benbecula is a gaff cutter, which was designed by Alexander Richardson and built by S. Bond & Co. in Birkenhead in 1897. StMSC member Bob Wilson and his family bought her in the mid-1960s and kept her in St Mawes. This photo shows her off Fowey in the late sixties with Bob's sons on board – Jimmy on the tiller and Robert on the foredeck – with two friends. In about 1973 the Wilsons sold her to John Green and Duggie Burnett, who then did a great deal of work on her. (The Wilson Collection)

John Sawle with Joe Andrew and Gus Southerd at Freshwater Boatyard in the 1960s. (The Sawle Collection)

Bomber Holm, who served as StMSC's Commodore from 2003 until 2011 – the second longest to do so – is seen here sailing his beloved Sunbeam *Clary*, which he owned for thirty-two years. (Jerome O'Hea)

Whim, one of Les Ferris's teaching/hire boats. (The Ferris Collection)

This photo was probably taken at Percuil in 1904 (some years before StMSC was formed) but it probably includes all five of the Falmouth 18 Foot Restricted Class built before then, two of which are still based in the Percuil River today. (StMSC Archive)

The Falmouth Working Boat *Victory* was built in 1884. For a brief time, in the early 1950s up until 1956, she had a Bermudan rig, as did one other Working Boat, *Maiden Nellie*. This was because there was very little Working Boat racing at that time and so these two boats had to try to compete against more modern yachts. This photo shows *Victory*, with a mainsail she had acquired from a 6-Metre, before the start of a regatta race at St Mawes. (The Banner Collection)

Dennis Edmonds was a member of StMSC from 1950 until his death in 2003. During this time he served on the committee for seven years and was briefly Vice Commodore and Rear Commodore. This photo shows him sailing his St Mawes One Design *John Dory* with his daughter Sheilagh, probably in 1964. He later owned the One Design *Choochky*, the last one built by Frankie Peters.
(The Banner Collection)

Dougie Sawle purchased the St Mawes OD *Curlew* in 1951 after he saw an advertisement in *Yachting World* saying she was for sale and lying on the Isle of Wight. He arranged for her to be brought home by train and he then owned her until 1975.
(The Sawle Collection)

In May 1997, StMSC hosted the most prestigious dinghy event in the club's history: the Laser II National Championships. Sixty-one boats took part in eight races – in predominantly moderate to fresh easterly winds in Falmouth Bay – over five days. (Brian Wheeldon)

The Penrose Trophy was originally donated by Dr N. C. Penrose OBE, who was Commodore from 1946 until 1949, and each year its recipient is decided by the incumbent Commodore. This photo shows Bomber Holm awarding it to John Bryant in 2004 'for his outstanding service to the Club as a Race Officer for many years'. (Mark Osborn)

Two boats on their way to overall victory in their 2006 Championships: David Liddington's *Athena* leading the Ajax fleet (above), and Charles Warren's Marieholm *Tringa* (below). (Both photos the Howard Collection)

The Pilot Cutter *Olga* was built in Porthleven in 1909. Between 1947 and 1975 she was owned by Colonel Pat Phibbs, who kept her in the Percuil River, and the photo above shows her sailing towards St Anthony's Head during that period. Since 1984 she has been owned by the Swansea Museum, and the photo below shows her racing from Fowey to St Mawes to take part in the Pilot Cutter Review in 2013, almost certainly the first time she had visited St Mawes for nearly forty years.
(The Southby-Tailyour Collection and Nigel Sharp)

Pilot Cutters moored off St Mawes in 2011 and starting a race in 2013.
(Nigel Sharp and Graham Pinkney)

Green Helix, the Twister owned by StMSC member Christopher Hoare from 2006 until 2013. Among Christopher's previous boats was *Ellida*, the very first GRP Nordic Folkboat, which he imported from Denmark himself. (The Hoare Collection)

Many club members have enjoyed the spectacle of *Grayhound* – a replica of a 1776 revenue cutter built in east Cornwall – which frequently visits St Mawes. She is seen here alongside the quay soon after she was completed in 2013. (Nigel Sharp)

Freddie (nearest the camera) and Ollie Grogono – the fifth generation of the Preston/Keith/Grogono family to join StMSC – sailing their Optimists towards Carricknath Point in 2010. For three years the brothers dominated the Optimist National Junior Championships: Ollie winning it in 2008, and Freddie in 2009 and 2010. Below they are pictured sailing together in a 29er in 2014. (Both photos Jeremy Grogono)

In September 2012 many StMSC members enjoyed the spectacle of a unique rowing event, when Cornwall's top female gig rowers accepted a challenge to race against eleven members of Team GB's highly successful Olympic women's rowing squad. The above photo, taken in the sailing club at the press briefing, includes three rowers who had won Olympic gold medals just a few months earlier: Katherine Grainger (extreme left), the Cornish-born Helen Glover (third from right) and Heather Stanning (second from right). Annie Vernon (also from Cornwall and the winner of an Olympic silver medal in 2008) organised the event and is nearest the camera. Three races took place, starting and finishing on StMSC's line, and the photo below shows the two Olympian boats at the back of the fleet in the second race in which Falmouth Ladies took the first two places. (Both photos Nigel Sharp)

In March 2015, on a day when the predicted height of low tide was -0.2 metres, an impromptu game of cricket took place on the exposed middle bank of the Percuil River involving several members of StMSC, including Commodore Nigel Sharp and Rear Commodore Sailing Mark Humphrey (and his dog Charlie). The playing regulations adopted for the game were questionable and the results were not recorded, but the wicket might have been described as 'sticky'.
(Graham Pinkney and the Sharp collection)

In 2013 *Gipsy Moth IV* – the ketch in which Francis Chichester famously sailed around the world single-handed, stopping just once – came to St Mawes and Falmouth. Since 2011 she has been owned by the Gipsy Moth Trust, whose aim is to protect and preserve her and 'enable as many people of all ages as is practicable to see her and sail her'. During the course of *Gipsy Moth's* fortnight in the area, a total of seventy-seven people got the chance to sail on her. Of the StMSC members who went, twelve didn't have to pay – their names were drawn out of a hat – thanks to the generosity of the Trust, who also kindly donated prizes for Junior Race Week. These photos show *Gipsy Moth* lying alongside in St Mawes and sailing in the Carrick Roads. (Both photos Nigel Sharp)

In 2013 StMSC member Charles Emmett competed in the OSTAR (the Original Single-handed Transatlantic Race) from Plymouth to Newport Rhode Island in his Sigma 36 *British Beagle*. His declared aim was just to finish the race – which he did after 27 days, 1 hour and 30 mins – and so he was delighted with his second place in the Jester Class, particularly as alternator problems meant that he had to steer for up to fifteen hours a day in the latter stages. This photo shows him nearing the finish. (Photo courtesy of the Royal Western YC)

In July 2015 Ian Matthews, grandson of StMSC's longest-serving Commodore, completed the Transatlantic Race from Newport, Rhode Island to the Lizard in his Pogo 12.5 *Jinja* in a time of 13 days, 8 hours, 36 minutes and 18 seconds. His crew were all members of StMSC – his sons Alex and Rupert, his son-in-law Jonathan Russell, Peter Shaw and Mike Hutton – and they are pictured here safely back on *Jinja's* mooring in the Percuil River the morning after finishing the race, with a bottle of champagne delivered by Peter's parents, Nick and Jo. (Jo Shaw)

In 2015 eleven boats competed in the annual Sunbeam Championships, the first ever to be hosted by StMSC. Six races were held over three days in Falmouth Bay, with the fleet returning to St Mawes at the end of each day. The photo above was taken soon after the start of the third race and the one below shows a carefully choreographed crossing of the StMSC line at the end of the Championships. (Nigel Sharp and John Howard)

St Mawes One Designs taking part in the seventy-fifth anniversary race in 1998 (above) and Percuil Regatta in 2003 (below). In June 1928 the *Falmouth Packet* reported that there were 'now three boats of the *Aileen* type and they should eventually make a very interesting one design class. They make very useful pleasure craft', and in August 1932, after the St Mawes Town Regatta, in which seven One Designs took part, that they were 'probably the best 16ft class in the country'. (Both photos StMOD Archive)